Walsingham
Prayer Book

Family Publications · Oxford

© Family Publications 2009

All rights reserved

ISBN 978-1-871217-93-3

Papal texts © Libreria Editrice Vaticana

picture credits
Br Lawrence Lew OP

acknowledgements
The publishers wish to thank Fr David Hartley,
Fr Joseph Welch Cong Orat and Fr Noel Wynn SM.

published by
Family Publications
Denis Riches House
66 Sandford Lane, Kennington,
Oxford, OX1 5RP
www.familypublications.co.uk

printed in England
through s|s|media limited

Table of Contents

Prayers

Our Lady of Walsingham	7
Prayer of Erasmus	9
Prayers of Blessing for Pilgrims	11
Prayer to Mary Queen of All Creation	13
Prayer at the Holy House	15
O Blessed Virgin Mary	17
A fifteenth-century Prayer	19
Litany of Our Lady of Walsingham	21
Prayer at the Feet of Our Lady of Walsingham	25
Prayer to Our Lady of Walsingham	27
Our Lady of Ransom	29
Visit to the Holy Ghost Chapel	31
Mary Star of Hope	33
Prayer for England	35
The Mysteries of the Rosary	36
The Angelus	39
Salve Regina	41
Regina Caeli	43

Hymns

Walsingham Pilgrim Hymn	44
In Splendour Arrayed	49
O Queen of the Holy Rosary	51
O Mother Blest	52
Ladye of Walsingham	53
Immaculate Mary	55
I'll Sing a Hymn to Mary	56
O Mother, dear Mother	57
Daily, Daily Sing to Mary	58
Mary of Walsingham	59
Ave Maris Stella	61
Hail Queen of Heaven	62
Lady of Walsingham	63
Consecration to Our Lady	64

*L*et us learn this from Mary our Mother. In England, "the Dowry of Mary", the faithful, for centuries, have made pilgrimage to her shrine at Walsingham. Today ... the statue of Our Lady of Walsingham, present here, lifts our minds to meditate on our Mother. She obeyed the will of God fearlessly and gave birth to the Son of God by the power of the Holy Spirit. Faithful at the foot of the Cross, she then waited in prayer for the Holy Spirit to descend on the infant Church. It is Mary who will teach us how to be silent, how to listen for the voice of God in the midst of a busy and noisy world. It is Mary who will help us to find time for prayer. Through the Rosary, that great Gospel prayer, she will help us to know Christ. We need to live as she did, in the presence of God, raising our minds and hearts to him in our daily activities and worries.

Pope John Paul II

Introduction

Pilgrims have been finding their way to Walsingham, England's national shrine of Our Lady, for the best part of 1000 years. Why do they travel to this small village in rural north Norfolk? For many visitors each year it is as tourists, for even more it is as pilgrims, but even for many of the casual visitors it is the beginning of a far more significant journey.

I first came to Walsingham in my teens, as part of a parish pilgrimage, and have been back many times since, to a place that changes little, while my life seems to change so much. Walsingham speaks of the eternal, but most importantly the entry into our time and space of the Creator of all. The eternal Word of God was born as a baby in a village to be our Saviour, and here in a small settlement the Saxon Lady of the Manor, Richeldis, received the news that she was to build a copy of the Holy House of Nazareth. Here a venerable image of Our Lady of Walsingham was enshrined, and began to attract pilgrims from all over Christendom. In time the whole village has grown to be a place of encounter with God, at Our Lady's invitation, as she shows us how we can be at home with God because he has made his home with us.

Our individual pilgrimages of life turn out to be part of something so much greater than our family, our parish. Our ups and downs of life and faith are set in a new perspective.

Whether you are on pilgrimage, in Walsingham, or at home, this book will provide prayers and hymns to give shape to your personal prayers, and will inspire you with its beautiful photographs.

Fr David Hartley, Sacred Heart parish, Oxford

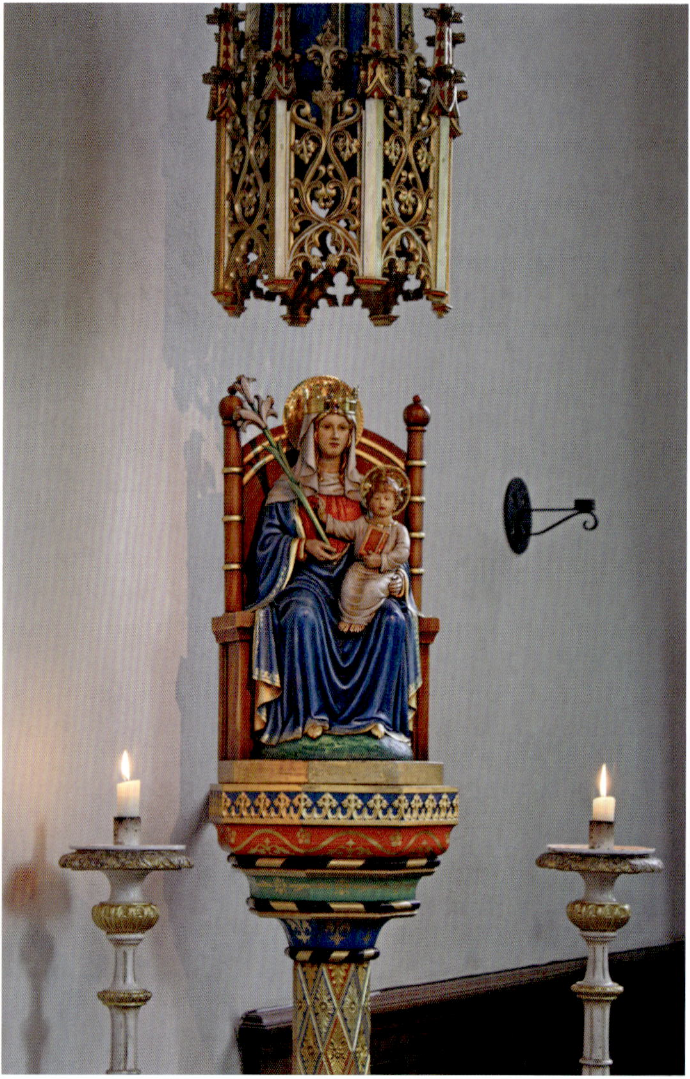

Our Lady of Walsingham

O Mary, recall the solemn moment
when Jesus, your divine Son,
dying on the cross confided us to your maternal care.

You are our Mother;
we desire ever to remain your devout children.

Let us therefore feel the effects
of your powerful intercession with Jesus Christ.

Make your name again glorious in this place,
once renowned throughout our land
by your visits, favours and many miracles.

Pray, O Holy Mother of God,
for the conversion of England,
restoration of the sick,
consolation for the afflicted,
repentance of sinners,
peace to the departed.

O Blessed Mary, Mother of God,
Our Lady of Walsingham intercede for us.

> Amen.

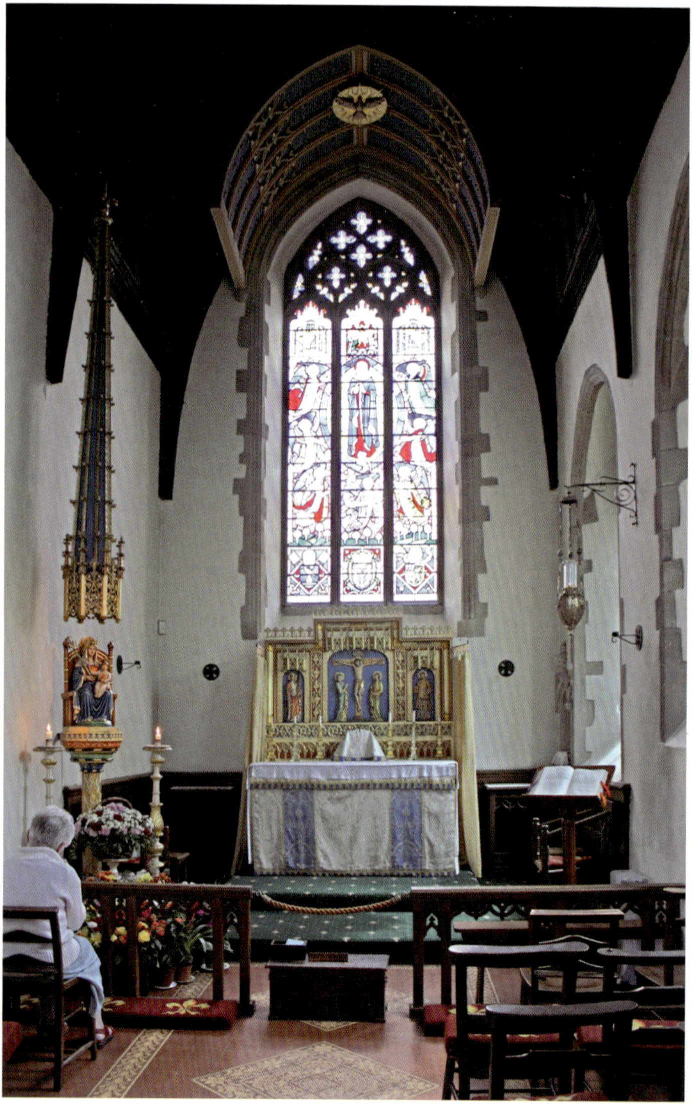

Prayer of Erasmus

O alone of all women, Mother and Virgin, Mother most blessed, Virgin most pure, now we sinful as we are, come to see thee who art all pure, we salute thee, we honour thee as how we may with our humble offerings; may thy Son grant us, that imitating thy most holy manners, we also, by the grace of the Holy Ghost, may deserve spiritually to conceive the Lord Jesus in our inmost soul, and once conceived, never to lose Him.

Amen.

From Erasmus' Vow to Our Lady of Walsingham

Hail! Jesus' Mother, blessed evermore,
Alone of women God-bearing and Virgin,
Others may offer to thee various gifts,
This man his gold, that man his silver.
A third adorns thy shrine with precious stones.
But this poor soul, bringing all he has,
Asks in reward for his most humble gift
That greatest blessing, piety of heart,
And free remission of his many sins.

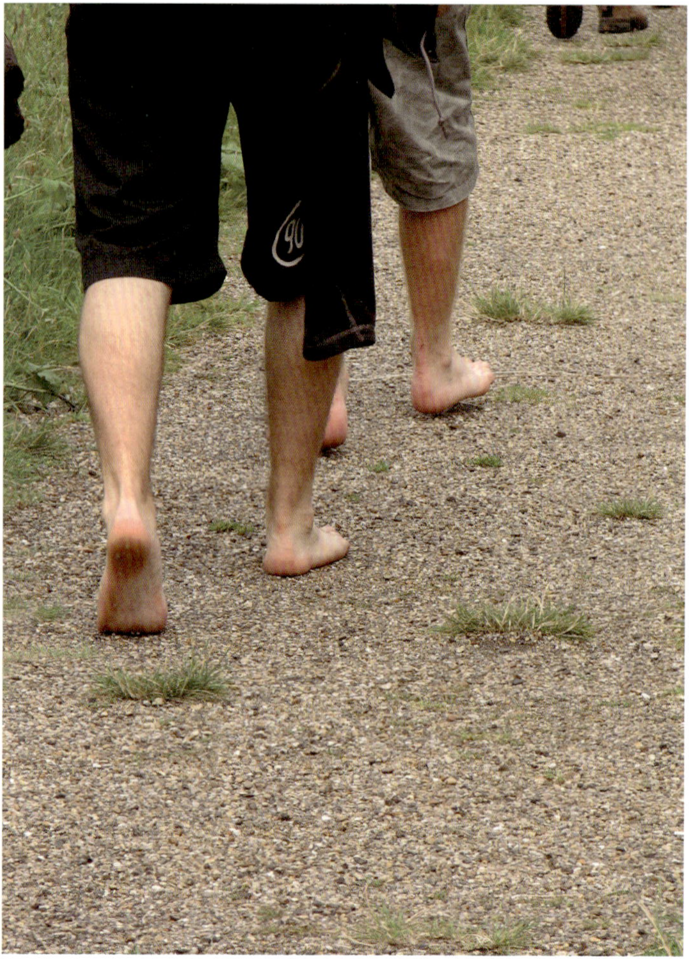

Prayers of Blessing for Pilgrims

⁖

All-powerful God,
you always show mercy towards those who love you and you are never far away from those who seek you. Remain with your servants on this holy pilgrimage and guide their way in accord with your will. Shelter them with your protection by day, give them the light of your grace by night, and, as their companion on the journey, bring them to their destination in safety.

Heavenly Father, who made the sons of Israel to walk with dry feet through the midst of the sea, and who did open to the three wise men, by the guiding of a star, the way that led to you; grant to us we beseech you, a safe journey and a time of tranquillity, that accompanied by your holy angel, we may arrive safely in Walsingham, and on return to our homes.
We ask this through Christ our Lord.

Amen.

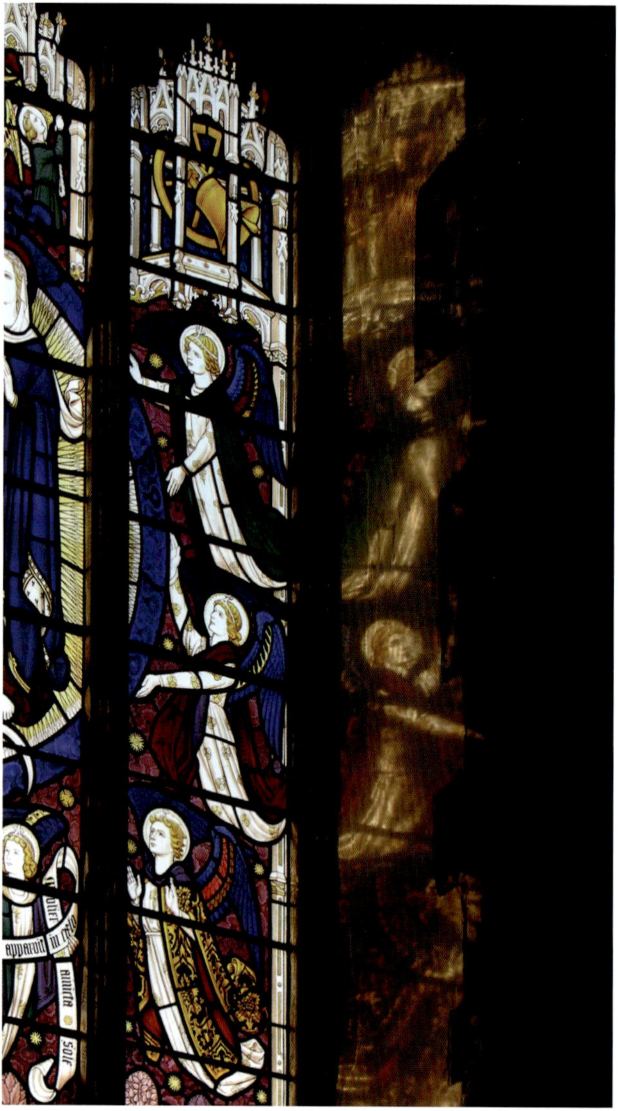
apparuit in celo
amicta
sole

Prayer to Mary Queen of All Creation

Finally, the Immaculate Virgin, preserved free from all guilt of original sin, on the completion of her earthly sojourn, was taken up body and soul into heavenly glory, and exalted by the Lord as Queen of all creation, that she might be the more fully conformed to her Son, the Lord of lords and the conqueror of sin and death.

Lumen Gentium 59

O Virgin Mary, Mother of God, you were taken up into heaven to be the beginning and the pattern of the Church in its perfection. You are a sign of hope and comfort for your people on their pilgrim way.

The God of all creation did not allow your body to be touched by decay, for you had given birth to His Son, Jesus the Lord of all life, in the glory of the Incarnation.

May you, Queen of all creation, teach us so to treasure life and care for the natural world, that we may honour the work of the Creator and be counted as good stewards of his Kingdom.

Amen.

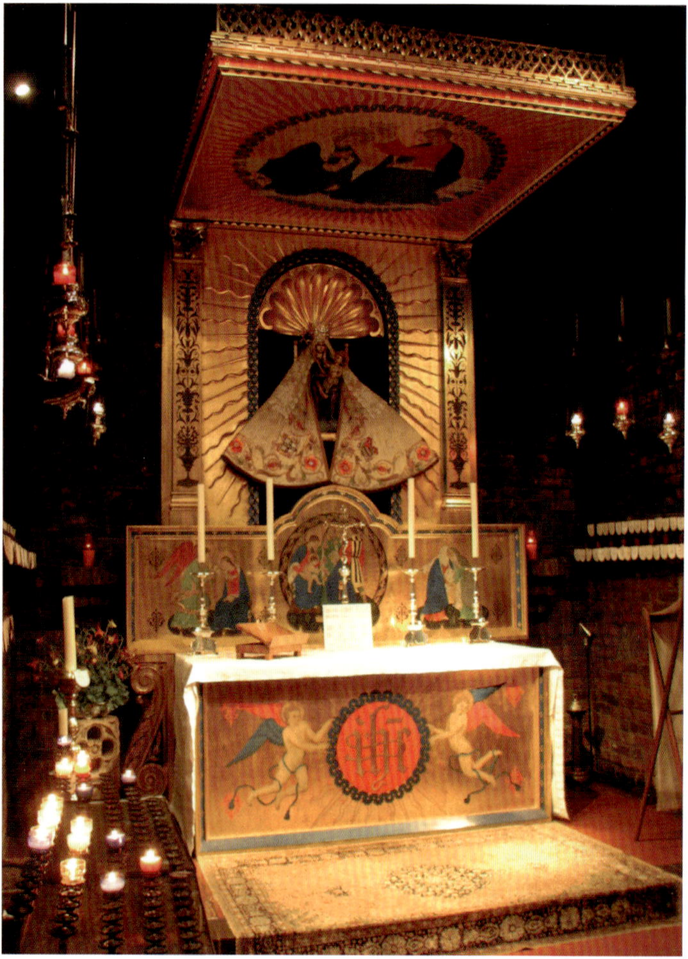

Prayer at the Holy House

☙☙

O Father Almighty, Who didst will that Thy Son our Lord Jesus Christ, the Eternal Word, should be incarnate of the Blessed Virgin Mary at the message of St Gabriel in the house of Nazareth, grant that we who visit this shrine of the house of the Annunciation, contemplating His humility and earthly poverty, may become truly humble, yet rich in grace, so that by His merits and the prayers of His holy Mother, we may become worthy of Thy Heavenly mansions. Through the same Jesus Christ our Lord, who lives and reigns for ever and ever.

Amen.

Act of Consecration

O Jesus, our Lord and Saviour, who didst live with Thy Mother in the Holy House at Nazareth, graciously accept the prayer I offer. I resolve to consecrate my whole life to Thy honour and that of Thy Blessed Mother, and by the power of the Holy Spirit will strive to hate sin, to accept suffering gladly and to be holy in thought, word and deed. Here in the Holy House, built at Thy Mother's command, I claim her prayers for me and join myself with all those who have honoured Thine Incarnation at England's Nazareth.

Amen.

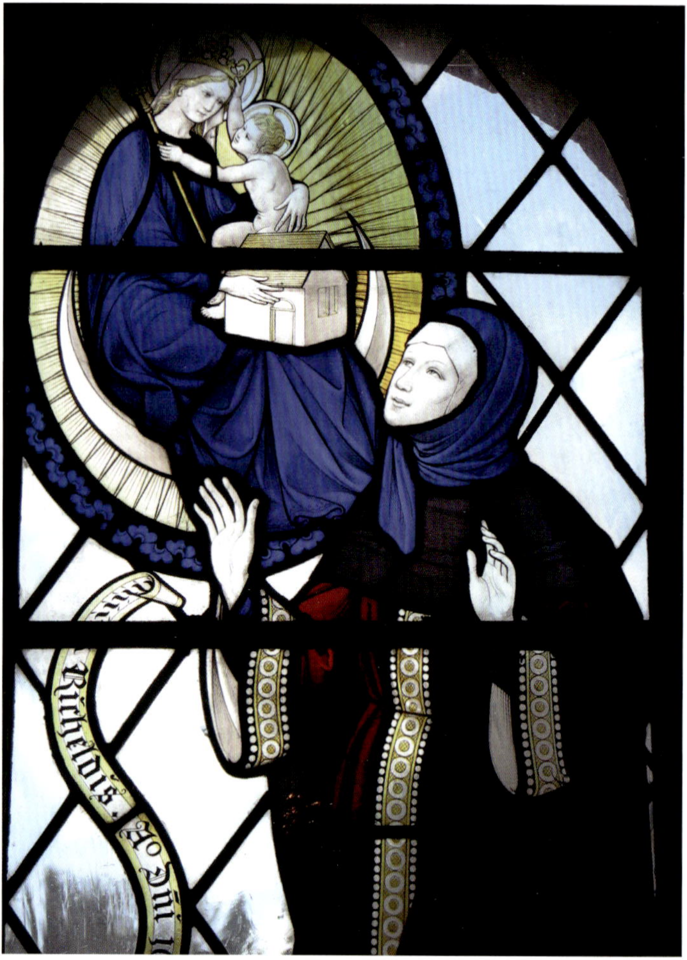
Richeldis

O Blessed Virgin Mary

O blessed Virgin Mary, Our Lady of Walsingham,
to thy loving intercession do we commend ourselves,
our homes and friends and our native land.
We recall with thankful hearts the love thou didst
show to thy Son on earth, and the blessings granted
us through thy prayers. As thy devoted children we
dedicate ourselves to His Service.
Our Lady of Walsingham, pray for us,
that whatsoever He saith unto us we may do it.

Amen.

Salve Mater Misericordiae

Dearest Mother, Mary most merciful
   Mother of God, Mary so pitiful,
   Mother of hope, Mother most beautiful,
   Mother of joy, holy and wonderful
   Mary, hear us.

   Mother of Jesus, Mary Comfortress,
   Be thou, dear Virgin, our true joyfulness
   And when we exiles end our weariness
   Grant us to share the Angels' blessedness,
   Mary, hear us.

Amen.

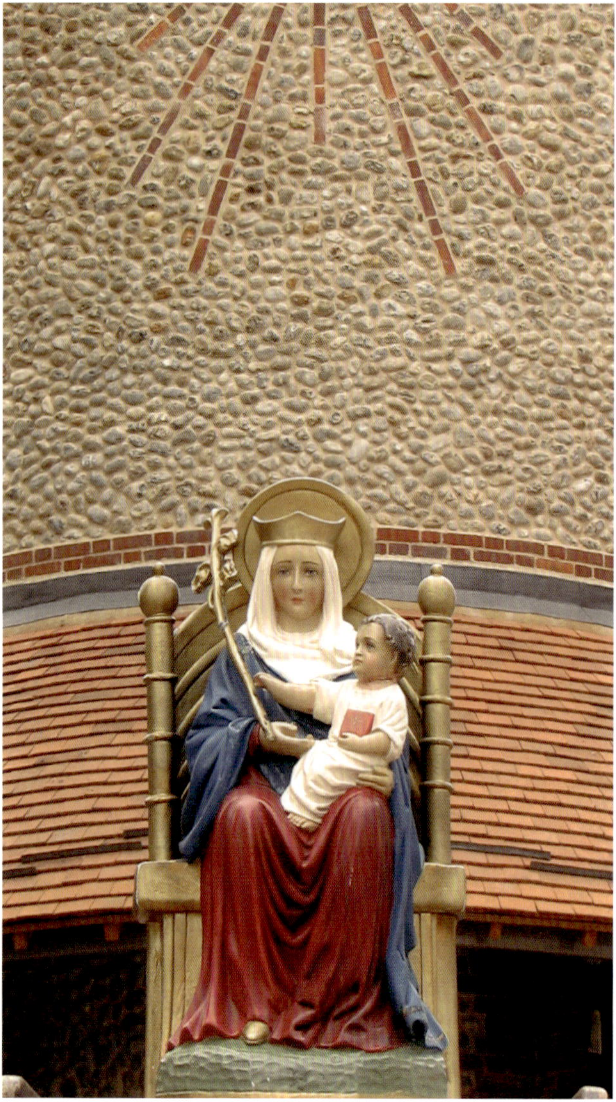

A fifteenth-century Prayer

O gracious Lady, glory of Jerusalem,
   Cypress of Sion and Joy of Israel,
   Rose of Jericho and Star of Bethlehem,
   O Gracious Lady our asking do not repel,
   In mercy all women ever thou dost excel,
   Therefore blessed Lady grant then thy great grace,
   To all that thee devoutly visit in this place.

   Amen.

The Memorare

Remember, O most loving Virgin Mary,
   that it is a thing unheard of, that anyone ever had
   recourse to your protection, implored your help,
   or sought your intercession, and was left forsaken.
   Filled therefore with confidence in your goodness
   I fly to you, O Mother, Virgin of virgins.
   To you I come, before you I stand,
   a sorrowful sinner.
   Despise not my poor words,
   O Mother of the Word of God,
   but graciously hear and grant my prayer.

   Amen.

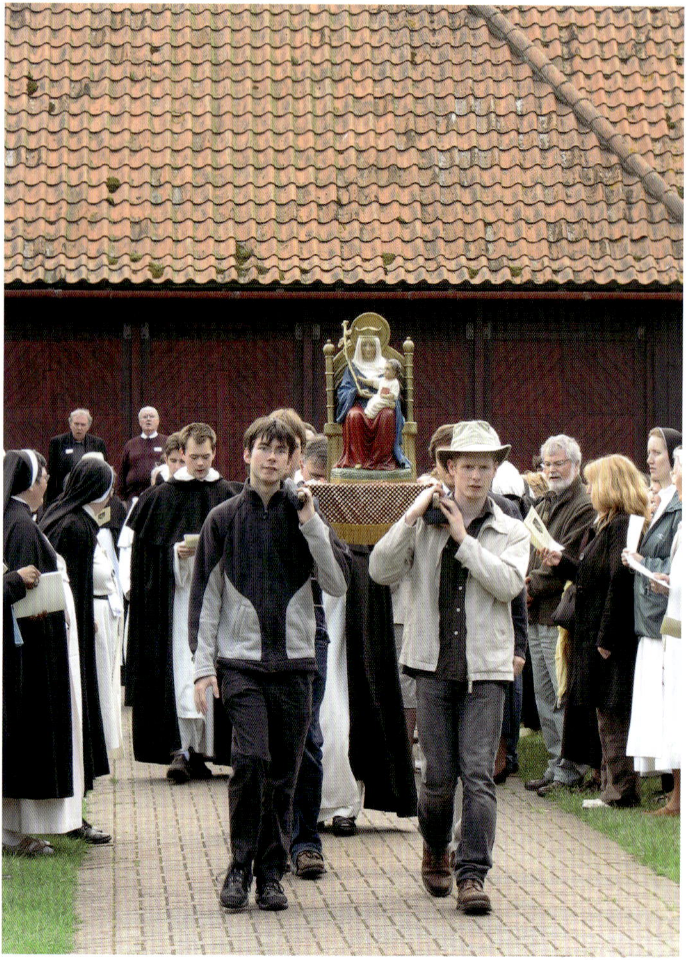

Litany of Our Lady of Walsingham

Mary *pray to the Lord for us.*
Mary, without sin, *pray to the Lord for us.*
Mary, God's Mother, *pray to the Lord for us.*
Mary the Virgin, *pray to the Lord for us.*
Mary taken to Heaven, *pray to the Lord for us.*

Mary at Bethlehem, *pray for all mothers.*
Mary at Nazareth, *pray for all families.*
Mary at Cana, *pray for all married couples.*
Mary at the Cross, *pray for all who suffer.*
Mary in the Upper Room, *pray for all who wait.*
Mary model of womanhood, *pray for all women.*

Woman of Faith, *keep us in mind.*
Woman of Hope, *keep us in mind.*
Woman of Charity, *keep us in mind.*
Woman of suffering, *keep us in mind.*
Woman of anxiety, *keep us in mind.*
Woman of humility, *keep us in mind.*
Woman of poverty, *keep us in mind.*
Woman of purity, *keep us in mind.*
Woman of obedience, *keep us in mind.*

Woman who wondered, *remember us to God.*
Woman who listened, *remember us to God.*

Woman who followed Him, *remember us to God.*
Woman who longed for Him, *remember us to God.*
Woman who loves Him, *remember us to God.*

Mother of God, *be our Mother always.*
Mother of Men, *be our Mother always.*
Mother of the Church, *be our Mother always.*
Mother of the World, *be our Mother always.*
Mother we need, *be our Mother always.*

Mother of the Unborn, *pray for all children.*

Mother who went on believing, *we thank God for you.*
Mother who never lost hope, *we thank God for you.*
Mother who loved to the end, *we thank God for you.*

> All Holy and ever-living God, in giving us Jesus Christ to be our Saviour and Brother, you gave us Mary, his Mother, to be our Mother also; grant us, we pray you, to live lives worthy of so great a Brother and so dear a Mother. May we come at last to you the Father of us all, through Jesus Christ your Son, who lives and reigns with you and the Holy Spirit for ever and ever.
>
> Amen.

Jesus, Mary and Joseph, I give you my heart and my soul.
Jesus, Mary and Joseph, assist me in my last agony.
Jesus, Mary and Joseph, may I breathe forth my soul in peace with you.

Our Lady of Walsingham, *pray for us.*

Let us pray

Father, give your people the joy of continual health in mind and body. With the prayers of the Virgin Mary to help us, guide us through this life to eternal happiness in the life to come. We ask this through Christ our Lord.

Amen.

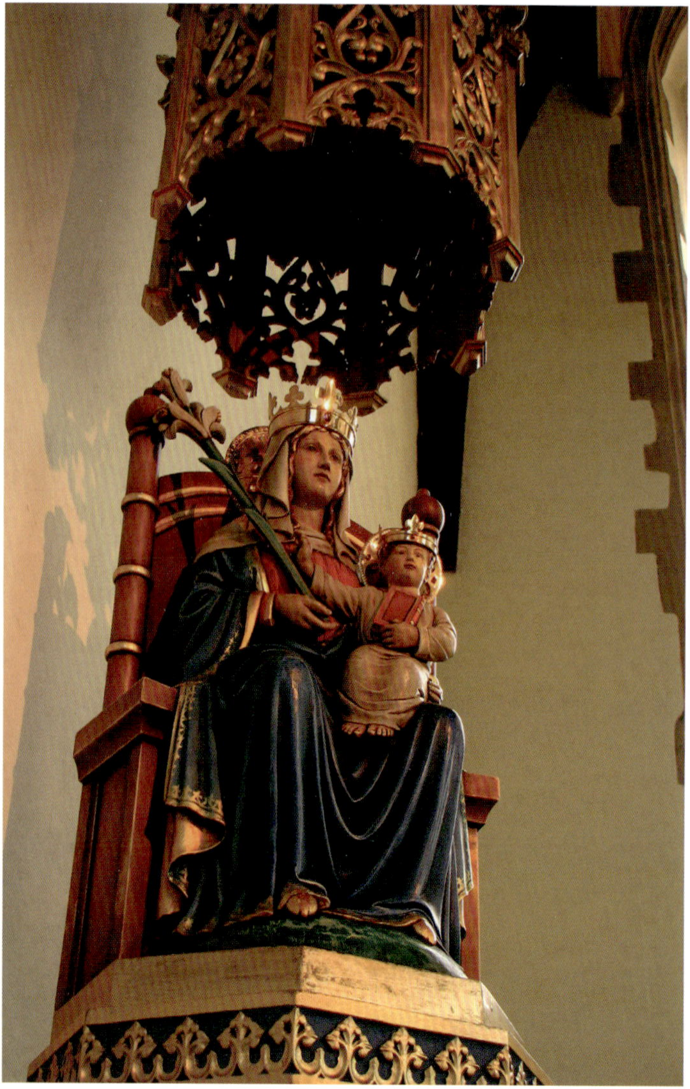

Prayer at the Feet of Our Lady of Walsingham

O Mary, O glorious Mother of my Saviour, behold me at my journey's end kneeling within this venerable sanctuary where, through the centuries, thou hast been the object of the devotion and confidence of the faithful. In this place where thy name is so great, thy protection so assured, where thou hast showered so many notable favours on those who have sought thy intercession, I humbly claim a share in thy prayers. O Mary, our Lady of Walsingham, I have undertaken this journey in order that I may obtain from thy Divine Son, our Lord Jesus Christ, through thy powerful intercession, the favour of ... (*name the request*)

Pray, dear Mother, that our Lord may make good all that is imperfect in my requests and obtain for me the crowning favour of a heart completely surrendered to his Will.

Amen.

O Lord God, Word Incarnate, Jesus of Nazareth, have mercy upon us. (*say three times*)
May the Divine Assistance remain always with us.

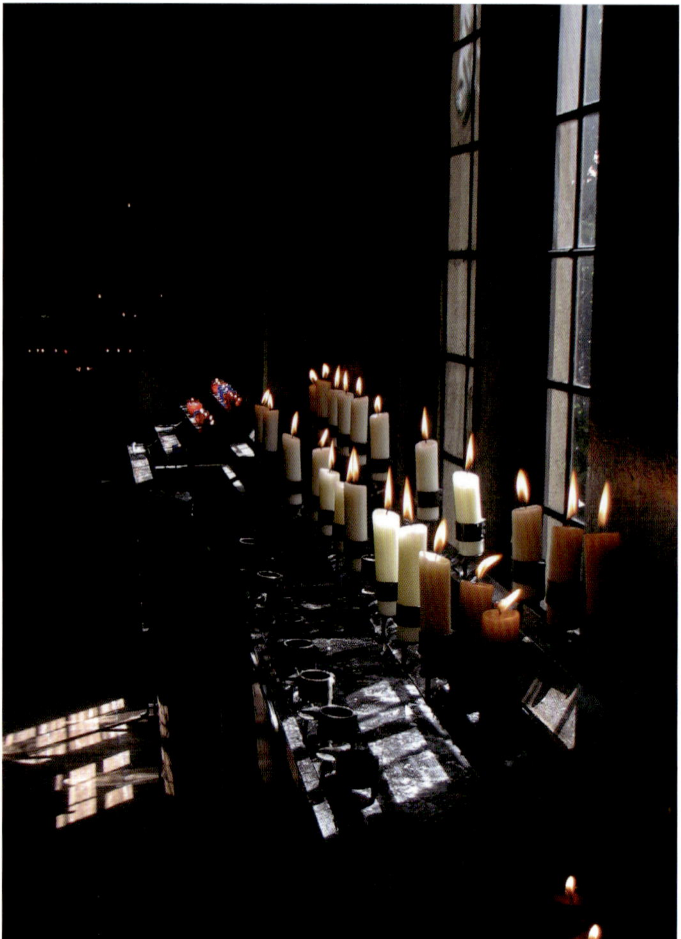

Prayer to Our Lady of Walsingham

Our Lady, who did ask for the Holy House to be built here in England, lead us to contemplate the hidden life of the Holy Family in Nazareth and to listen to the voice of God in the stillness of our hearts. May we find sanctuary in your maternal care and comfort in your prayers. Guide us on this pilgrimage on earth, that, by imitating your joyful welcome of the divine will, we too may one day dwell with the Blessed Trinity for ever.

Amen.

Lord God, in the mystery of the Incarnation
Mary conceived your Son in her heart
before she conceived him in her womb.
As we, your pilgrim people, rejoice in her patronage,
grant that we also may welcome him into our hearts,
and so, like her, be made a holy house fit for his eternal
dwelling. We ask this through our Lord Jesus Christ,
your Son who lives and reigns with you in the unity of
the Holy Spirit, God for ever and ever.

Amen.

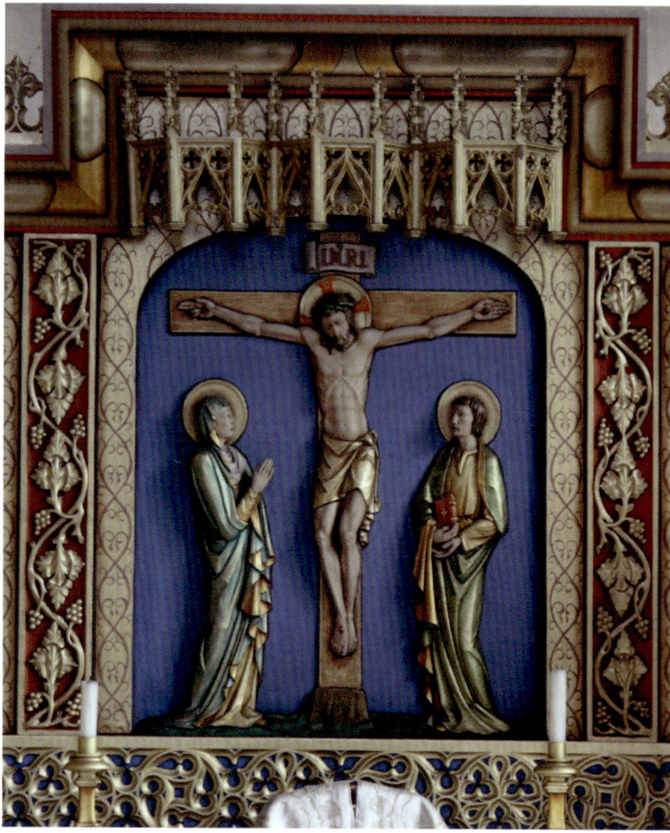
INRI

Our Lady of Ransom

Lord,
 We have long been the Dowry of Mary
 and subjects of Peter, Prince of the Apostles.
 Let us hold to the Catholic Faith
 and remain devoted to the Blessed Virgin
 and obedient to Peter.
 We ask this through Our Lord Jesus Christ, your Son,
 who lives and reigns with you and the Holy Spirit,
 one God, for ever and ever.

> Amen.

Sub tuum Praesidium

We fly to thy protection,
 O holy Mother of God;
 despise not our petitions
 in our necessities,
 but deliver us always
 from all dangers,
 O glorious and blessed Virgin.

> Amen.

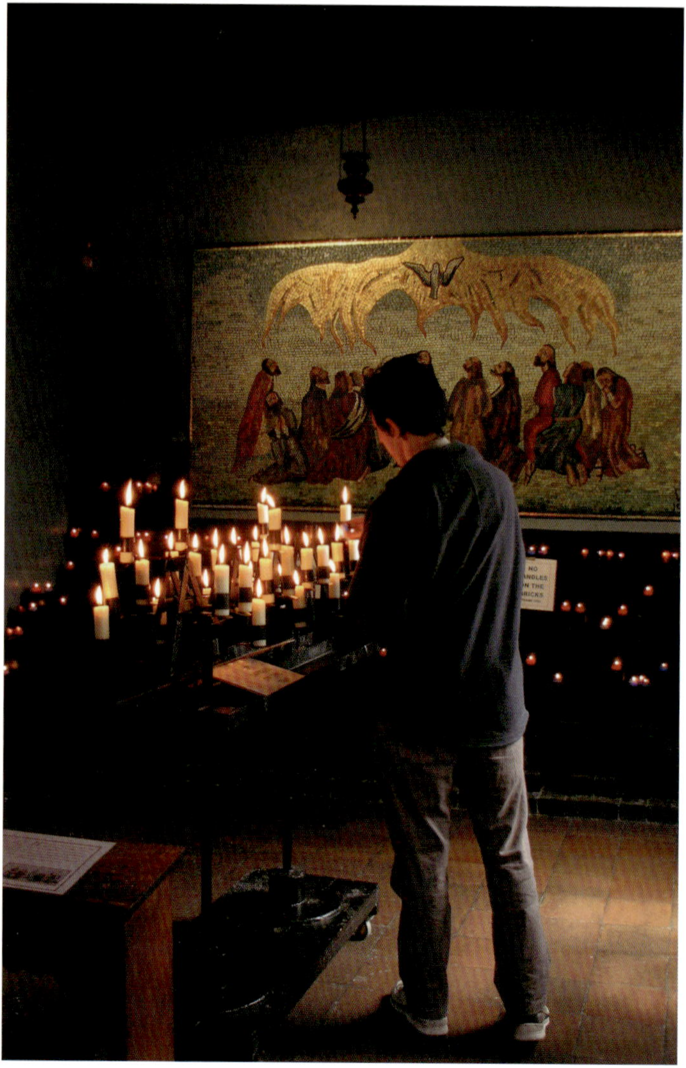

Visit to the Holy Ghost Chapel

☙❧

I am going to reveal to you the secret to sanctity and happiness. If every day during five minutes, you will silence your imagination, close your eyes to things of sense and your ears to earthly sounds in order to enter into yourself and there in the sanctuary of your baptized soul, which is the temple of the Holy Spirit, speak to this Divine Spirit and say:

"O Holy Spirit, Soul of my soul I adore You. Enlighten, guide, strengthen and console me; tell me what I should do; give me Your orders. I promise to be submissive in all that You desire of me and to accept all that You allow to happen to me. Grant only to me to know Your will."

If you do this you will pass your life happily, serene and consoled, even in the midst of pains, because grace will be in proportion to your trials giving you strength to bear them. Thus you will arrive at the Gates of Heaven full of merit. This submission to the Holy Spirit is the secret of sanctity.

Cardinal Mercier (1851-1926)
Written by him from the Holy Ghost Chapel
in the Slipper Chapel in Walsingham

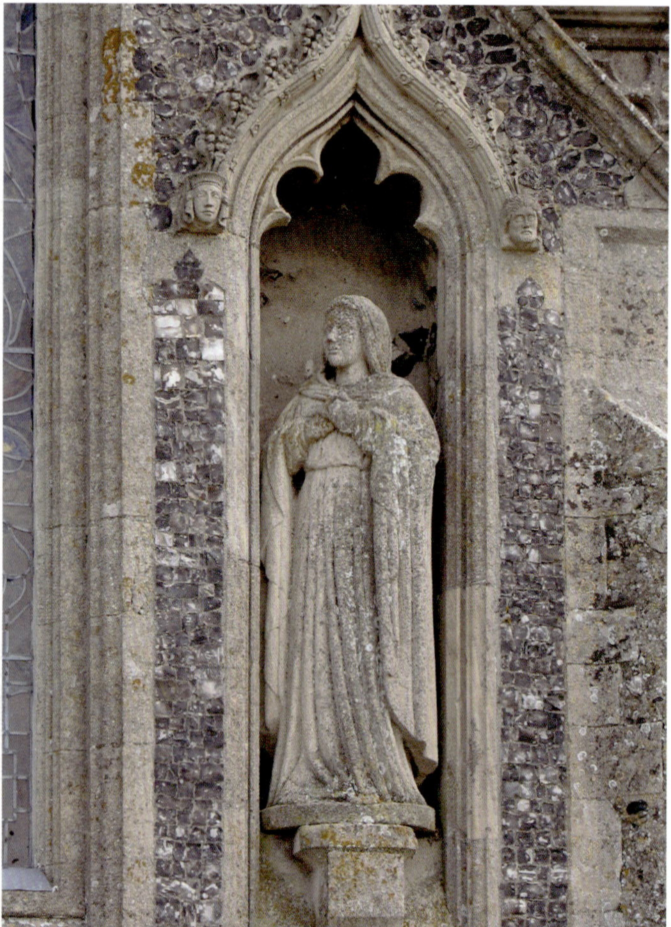

Mary Star of Hope

With a hymn composed in the eighth or ninth century, thus for over a thousand years, the Church has greeted Mary, the Mother of God, as "Star of the Sea": *Ave maris stella*. Human life is a journey. Towards what destination? How do we find the way? Life is like a voyage on the sea of history, often dark and stormy, a voyage in which we watch for the stars that indicate the route. The true stars of our life are the people who have lived good lives. They are lights of hope. Certainly, Jesus Christ is the true light, the sun that has risen above all the shadows of history. But to reach him we also need lights close by – people who shine with his light and so guide us along our way. Who more than Mary could be a star of hope for us? With her "yes" she opened the door of our world to God himself; she became the living Ark of the Covenant, in whom God took flesh, became one of us, and pitched his tent among us (cf. Jn 1:14).

Holy Mary, Mother of God, our Mother, teach us to believe, to hope, to love with you. Show us the way to his Kingdom! Star of the Sea, shine upon us and guide us on our way!

Pope Benedict XVI, Spe Salvi

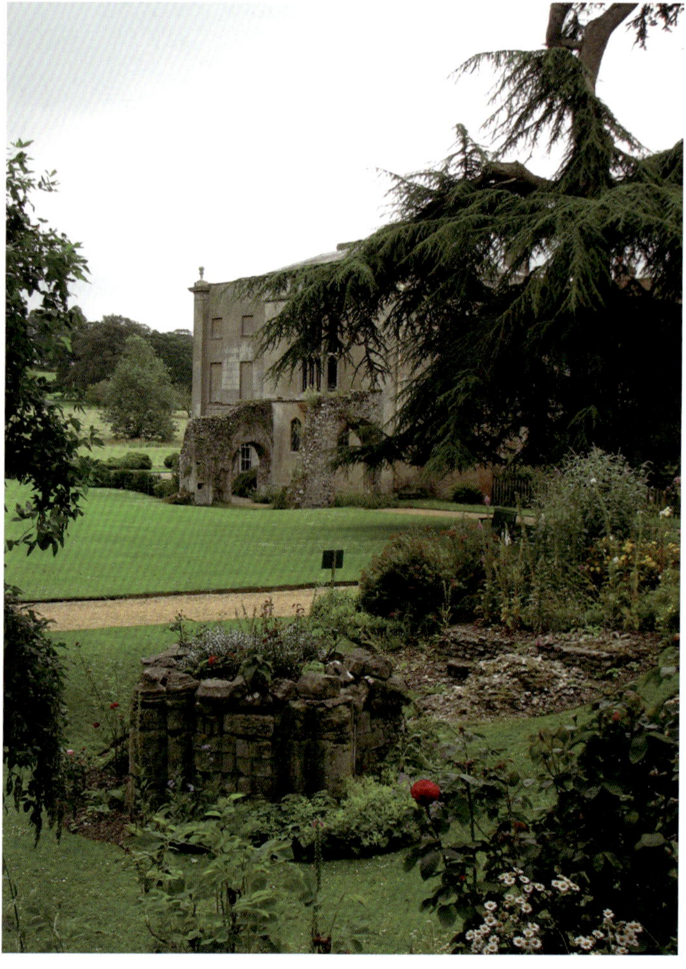

Prayer for England

O Blessed Virgin Mary, Mother of God,
and our most gentle Queen and Mother,
look down in mercy upon England, thy dowry;
and upon us all who greatly hope and trust in thee.
By thee it was that Jesus, our Saviour and our hope,
was given unto the world; and he has given thee to us
that we may hope still more.
Plead for us thy children, whom thou didst receive
and accept at the foot of the cross,
O sorrowful Mother.
Intercede for our separated brethren, that with us
in the one true fold, they may be united to
the chief Shepherd, the Vicar of thy Son.
Pray for us all, dear Mother,
that by faith, fruitful in good works
we may all deserve to see and praise God,
together with thee in our heavenly home.

Amen.

The Mysteries of the Rosary

The Joyful Mysteries

1. The Annunciation (Lk 1:26-38).
2. The Visitation (Lk 1:39-56).
3. The Nativity (Lk 2:1-7).
4. The Presentation in the Temple (Lk 2:22-39).
5. The Finding of the Child Jesus in the Temple (Lk 2:41-52).

The Luminous Mysteries

1. The Baptism of Christ in the Jordan (Mt 3:13-17).
2. The Wedding Feast at Cana (Jn 2:1-12).
3. The Proclamation of the Kingdom (Mk 1:14-15; 2:1-12).
4. The Transfiguration (Lk 9:28-36).
5. The Institution of the Eucharist (Mt 26:26-29).

The Sorrowful Mysteries

1. The Agony of Christ in the Garden (Mk 14:32-42).
2. The Scourging at the Pillar (Mt 27:15-26).
3. The Crowning with Thorns (Mt 27:27-31).
4. The Carrying of the Cross (Jn 19:15-17; Lk 23:27-32).
5. The Crucifixion of Jesus (Lk 23:33-46).

The Glorious Mysteries

1. The Resurrection of Jesus (Mt 28:1-8).
2. The Ascension of Jesus into Heaven (Ac 1:6-11).
3. The Descent of the Holy Spirit (Ac 2:1-12).
4. The Assumption of Mary into Heaven (1 Cor 15:20-23).
5. The Coronation of Our Lady in Heaven (Rev 12:1; 14:1-5).

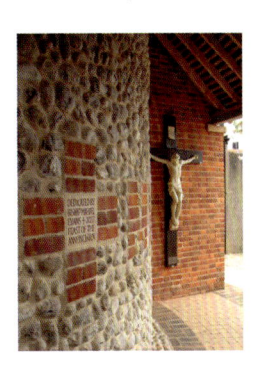

AVE MARIA
GRATIA
PLENA

The Angelus

℣. The Angel of the Lord declared unto Mary,
℟. And she conceived of the Holy Spirit.

Hail Mary, full of grace, the Lord is with thee. Blessed art thou among women and blessed is the fruit of thy womb, Jesus.

Holy Mary, Mother of God, pray for us sinners, now, and at the hour of our death. Amen

℣. Behold the handmaid of the Lord,
℟. Be it done unto me according to Thy word.

Hail Mary, ...

℣. And the Word was made flesh,
℟. And dwelt among us.

Hail Mary, ...

℣. Pray for us, O holy Mother of God,
℟. That we may be made worthy of the promises of Christ.

Let us pray

Pour forth, we beseech Thee, O Lord, Thy grace into our hearts; that we, to whom the Incarnation of Christ Thy Son was made known by the message of an Angel, may, by His Passion and Cross, be brought to the glory of His Resurrection. Through the same Christ our Lord.

Amen.

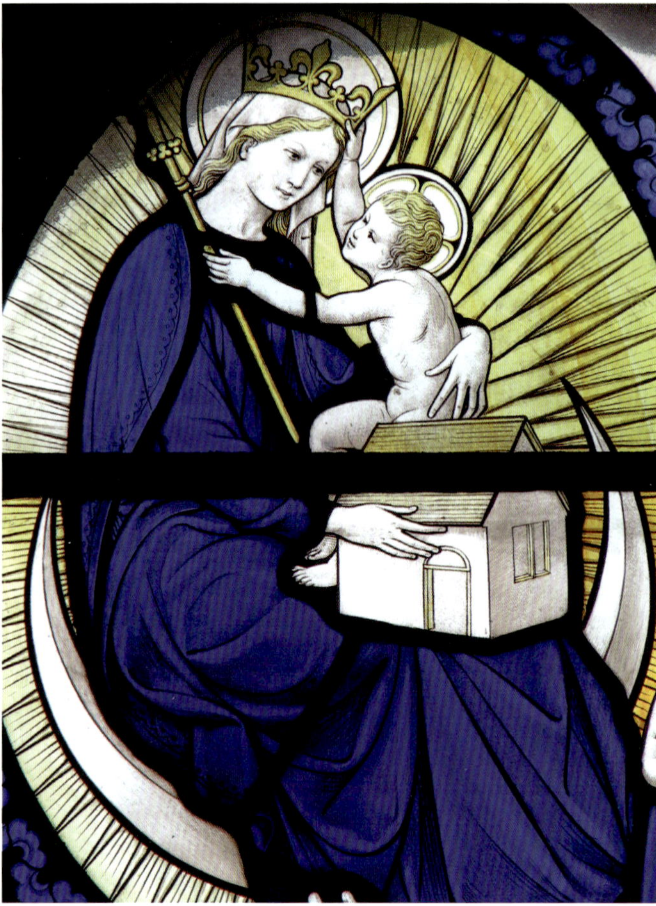

Salve Regina

Salve Regina, Mater misericordiae,
vita, dulcedo, et spes nostra, salve.
Ad te clamamus, exsules filii Evae,
ad te suspiramus, gementes et flentes
in hac lacrimarum valle.
Eia, ergo, advocata nostra, illos tuos
misericordes oculos ad nos converte;
et Jesum, benedictum fructum ventris tui,
nobis post hoc exilium ostende.
O clemens, O pia, O dulcis Virgo Maria.

Hail Holy Queen, Mother of mercy,
Hail our life, our sweetness, and our hope.
To thee do we cry, poor banished children of Eve.
To thee do we send up our sighs
mourning and weeping in this vale of tears.
Turn then, most gracious advocate,
thine eyes of mercy towards us,
and after this our exile show unto us
the blessed fruit of thy womb, Jesus.
O clement, O loving, O sweet Virgin Mary.

℣. Pray for us, O holy Mother of God.
℟. That we may be made worthy of the promises of Christ.

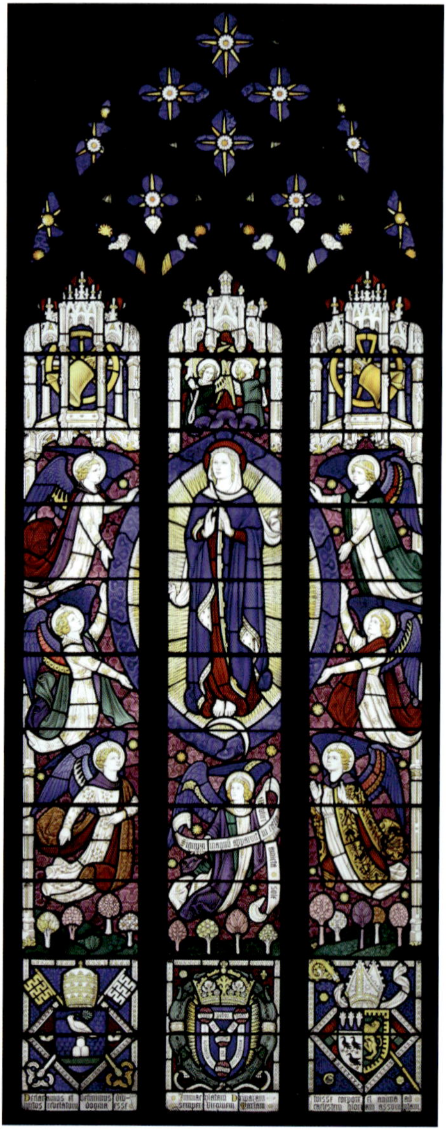

Regina Caeli

Regina caeli, laetare, alleluia:
　Quia quem meruisti portare, alleluia,
　Resurrexit, sicut dixit, alleluia.
　Ora pro nobis Deum, alleluia.

℣. Gaude et laetare, Virgo Maria, alleluia.
℟. Quia surrexit Dominus vere, alleluia.

Queen of heaven, rejoice, alleluia:
　For He whom you did merit to bear, alleluia,
　Has risen, as He said, alleluia.
　Pray for us to God, alleluia.

℣. Rejoice and be glad, O Virgin Mary, alleluia.
℟. For the Lord has truly risen, alleluia.

Let us pray

O God, who gave joy to the world through the resurrection of your Son, our Lord Jesus Christ, grant we beseech you, that through the intercession of the Virgin Mary, his Mother, we may obtain the joys of everlasting life. Through the same Christ our Lord.

　　　　　　　　　　　　　　　Amen.

Walsingham Pilgrim Hymn

All Glory to God in His mercy and grace
Who hath stablished His home in this wonderful place.
Ave, Ave, Ave Maria! Ave, Ave, Ave Maria!

All Glory to Jesus our Saviour and Lord
Whose image within us by grace is restored. *Ave, ...*

All Glory to God in His Spirit Divine
Who hath fixed His abode in this poor soul of mine. *Ave, ...*

Sing the praises of Mary, the Mother of God
Whose 'Walsingham Way' countless pilgrims have trod. *Ave, ...*

Then lift high your voices, rehearse the glad tale
of our Lady's appearing in Stiffkey's fair vale. *Ave, ...*

When Edward Confessor ruled over the land
The Faverche's Manor stood here nigh at hand. *Ave, ...*

The Lady Richeldis devoted her care
to good works and penance and worship and prayer. *Ave, ...*

One day as she prayed and looked up to the skies,
A vision of splendour delighted her eyes. *Ave, ...*

Our Lady, God's Mother, in glory arrayed,
Held a house in her arms which was clearly displayed. *Ave, ...*

Take note my dear daughter, and build here a shrine,
As Nazareth's home in this country of thine. *Ave, ...*

And the spot that I choose where the house shall arise
By a sign shall be plainly revealed to your eyes. *Ave, ...*

The vision passed slowly away from her sight
But her mind held the house in its length, breadth and height. *Ave, ...*

Bewildered she pondered this message so sweet,
When a clear spring of water burst forth at her feet. *Ave, ...*

Bewildered no longer for this was the sign,
She vowed on this spot she would build such a shrine. *Ave, ...*

The finest materials her workmen could find
She employed for this house she had fixed in her mind. *Ave, ...*

But though she had given both timbers and lands,
The power of the work lay in Mary's own hands. *Ave, ...*

And this was made clear when the work was complete
By the answers to prayers poured out at her feet. *Ave, ...*

And soon mighty wonders by Grace were revealed,
For the sick who made use of the waters were healed. *Ave, ...*

So Walsingham then came a place of great fame,
and Our Lady herself was called by this name. *Ave, ...*

And many a pilgrim to the day of his death,
Took the road once a year to England's Nazareth. *Ave, ...*

So crowded were roads that the stars, people say,
That shine in the heavens were called 'Walsingham Way'. *Ave, ...*

And many the favours and graces bestowed
On those, who in faith, took the pilgrimage road. *Ave, ...*

The image of Mary with her Holy Son
Was honoured and feted by everyone. *Ave, ...*

The Canons and Friars built houses around
And the praises of God were a regular sound. *Ave, ...*

And Kings, Lords and Commons their homage would pay
And the burning of tapers turned night into day. *Ave, ...*

But at last came a King who had greed in his eyes,
And he lusted for treasure with fraud and with lies. *Ave, ...*

The order went forth; and with horror 'twas learned.
That the shrine was destroyed and the image was burned. *Ave, ...*

And here where God's mother had once been enthroned,
The souls that stayed faithful 'neath tyranny groaned. *Ave, ...*

And this realm which had once been our Lady's own Dower
Had its church now enslaved by the secular power. *Ave, ...*

And so dark night fell on this glorious place
Where all former glories there hardly was trace. *Ave, ...*

Yet a thin stream of pilgrims still walked the old way
And hearts longed to see this night turned into day. *Ave, ...*

Till at last, when full measure of penance was poured,
In her Shrine see the honour of Mary restored. *Ave, ...*

Again, 'neath her image the tapers shine fair
In her children's endeavours past wrongs to repair. *Ave, ...*

Again in her house due honour is taught;
Her name is invoked, her fair graces besought. *Ave, ...*

And the sick and the maimed seek the pilgrimage way,
And miraculous healing their bodies display. *Ave, ...*

Oh, Mother give heed to the prayer of our heart,
that your glory from here never more may depart. *Ave, ...*

Now to God the All-Father, and Son, with due praise,
And life giving Spirit, thanksgiving we raise. *Ave, ...*

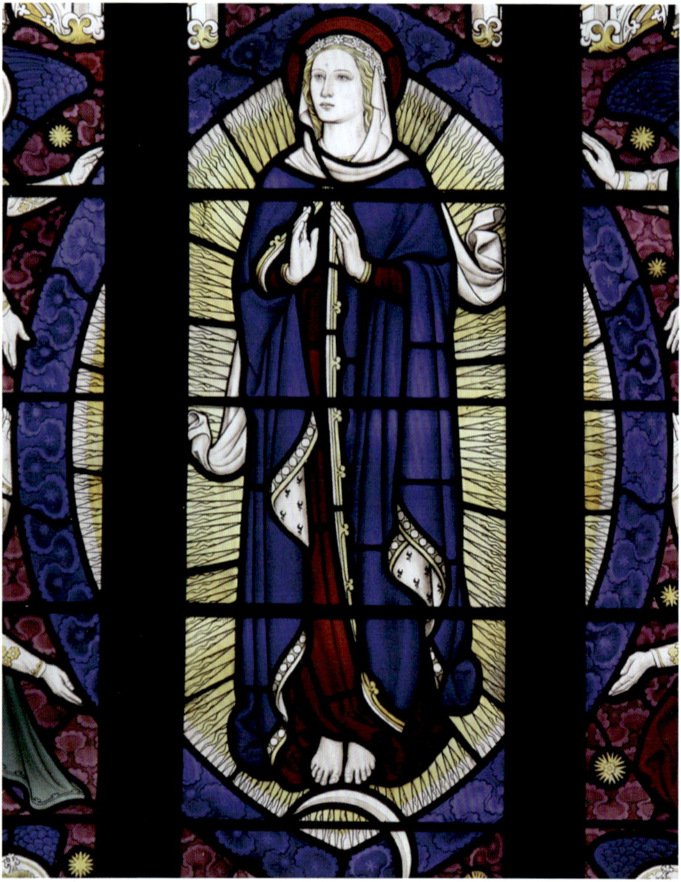

In Splendour Arrayed

In splendour arrayed,
In vesture of gold,
The Mother of God
In glory behold!
O Daughter of David,
Thou dwellest on high,
Excelling in brightness
The hosts of the sky.

O Maiden thou art
A Mother renowned;
A Mother who yet
As Virgin art crowned;
The Lord of the Angels,
God high and supreme,
Took flesh of thy substance,
The world to redeem.

All kindreds and tongues
Thine Offspring adore,
Creation must bow
His footstool before;
At thy gentle pleadings
May he from his height
Disperse all our shadows
And fill us with light.

The Father we praise,
Who chose for his Son
A Mother all-pure,
Th'immaculate one.
All praise to her offspring
Who saveth our race;
Like praise to the Spirit,
Who filled her with grace.

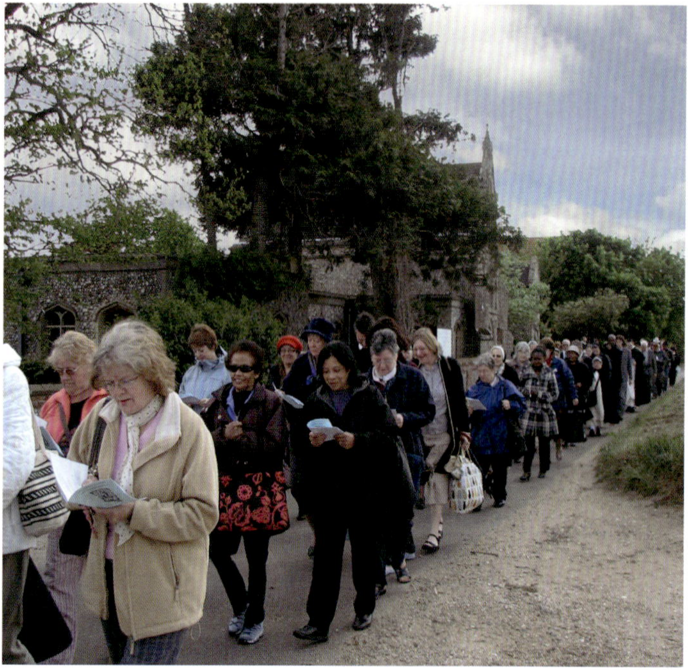

O Queen of the Holy Rosary

O Queen of the Holy Rosary,
O bless us as we pray,
And offer thee our roses
In garlands day by day,
While from our Father's garden,
With loving hearts and bold,
We gather to thine honour
Buds white and red and gold.

O Queen of the Holy Rosary,
Each myst'ry blends with thine
The sacred life of Jesus
In ev'ry step divine.
Thy soul was His fair garden,
Thy virgin breast His throne,
Thy thoughts His faithful mirror,
Reflecting Him alone.

Sweet Lady of the Rosary,
White roses let us bring,
And lay them round thy footstool,
Before our Infant King.
For, resting in thy bosom,
God's Son was fain to be
The Child of thy obedience
And spotless purity.

O Mother Blest

O Mother blest, whom God bestows
 On sinners and on just
What joy, what hope thou givest those
 Who in thy mercy trust.

> *Thou art clement, thou art chaste,*
> *Mary, thou art fair;*
> *Of all mothers sweetest, best;*
> *None with thee compare.*

O heavenly Mother, mistress sweet!
It never yet was told
That suppliant sinner left thy feet
Unpitied, unconsoled.

O Mother, pitiful and mild,
Cease not to pray for me;
For I do love thee as a child,
And sigh for love of thee.

Most powerful Mother, all men know
Thy Son denies thee nought;
Thou askest, wishest it, and lo!
His power thy will hath wrought.

O Mother blest, for me obtain,
Ungrateful though I be,
To love that God who first could deign
To show such love for me.

Ladye of Walsingham

Joy to thee, Queen, within thine ancient dowry –
joy to thee, Queen, for once again thy fame
is noised abroad and spoken of in England
and thy lost children call upon thy name.

> *Ladye of Walsingham, be as thou hast been –*
> *England's Protectress, our Mother and our Queen!*

In ages past, thy palmer-children sought thee
from near and far, a faith-enlightened throng,
bringing their gems, and gold and silver love-gifts
where tapers gleamed, where all was prayer and song.

Countless the signs and wonders that men told there,
for not in vain did any pilgrim kneel
before thy throne to seek thy intercession
but thou didst bend to listen and to heal.

The Martyrs' blood, like heavenly seed, is scattered;
the harvest now is ripe for us to reap;
the Faith dishonoured now is held in honour;
O help thine own this precious gift to keep!

Unto thy Son – unto our sweet Redeemer,
Source of our Hope, our Life, our Joy, once more
we bring the love and loyalty of England
and in his Sacrament we him adore.

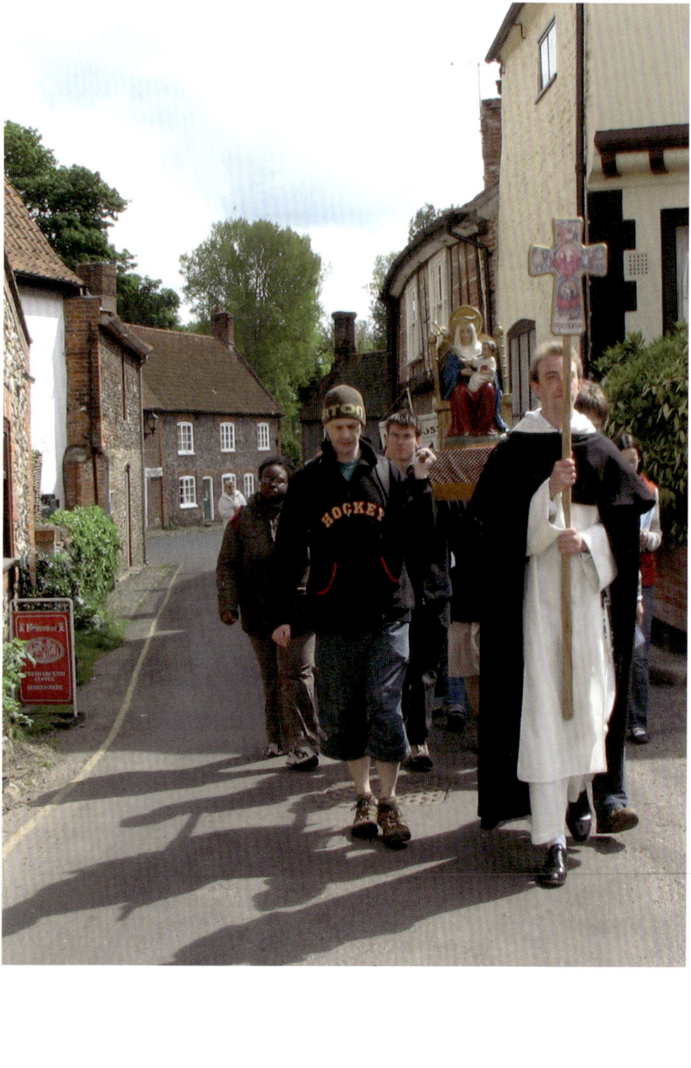
HOCKEY

Immaculate Mary

Immaculate Mary!
Our hearts are on fire,
That title so wondrous
Fills all our desire.

Ave, ave, ave, Maria! (2)

We pray for God's glory,
May His Kingdom come!
We pray for His Vicar,
Our Father, and Rome.

Ave ...

We pray for our Mother
The Church upon earth,
And bless, sweetest Lady,
The land of our birth.

Ave ...

For poor, sick, afflicted
thy mercy we crave;
and comfort the dying
thou light of the grave.

Ave ...

There is no need, Mary,
nor ever has been,
which thou canst not succour,
Immaculate Queen.

Ave ...

In grief and temptation,
in joy or in pain,
we'll ask thee, our Mother,
nor seek thee in vain.

Ave ...

O bless us, dear Lady,
With blessings from heaven.
And to our petitions
Let answer be given.

Ave ...

In death's solemn moment,
our Mother, be nigh;
as children of Mary
O teach us to die.

Ave ...

And crown thy sweet mercy
With this special grace,
To behold soon in heaven
God's ravishing face.

Ave ...

Now to God be all glory
And worship for aye,
And to God's virgin Mother
An endless Ave.

Ave ...

I'll Sing A Hymn to Mary

I'll sing a hymn to Mary,
  The Mother of my God,
  The Virgin of all virgins,
  Of David's royal blood.
  O teach me Holy Mary,
  A loving song to frame,
  When wicked men blaspheme thee
  To love and bless thy name.

O lily of the Valley,
  O mystic Rose, what tree,
  Or flower, e'en the fairest,
  Is half so fair as Thee?
  O let me tho' so lowly
  Recite my Mother's fame,
  When wicked men blaspheme thee,
  I'll love and bless thy name.

O noble Tower of David,
  Of gold and ivory.
  The Ark of God's own promise,
  The gate of Heav'n to me.
  To live and not to love thee
  Would fill my soul with shame;
  When wicked men blaspheme thee,
  I'll love and bless thy name.

The saints are high in glory,
  With golden crowns so bright;
  But brighter far is Mary,
  Upon her throne of light.
  Oh that which God did give thee,
  Let mortal ne'er disclaim;
  When wicked men blaspheme thee,
  I'll love and bless thy name.

But in the crown of Mary,
  There lies a wonderous gem,
  As Queen of all the angels,
  Which Mary shares with them;
  No sin hath e'er defiled thee,
  So doth our faith proclaim;
  When wicked men blaspheme thee,
  I'll love and bless thy name.

O Mother, dear Mother

O Mother, dear Mother
We flock to thy throne
We come from the kingdom
That once was thine own.

For England in old time
Thy Dowry was called
Till spoiled by the spoiler
Till captive enthralled.

Then Jesus our King was
Supreme in the land,
And thou the Queen-Mother
Reigned at His right hand.

Then every fair altar
was throne for our King
While priest, peer and peasant
His praises would sing.

And when the glad feasts
Of our Lady came round,
The streets of each town
Would her praises resound.

The guilds made procession
To Honour their Queen
The banners shone forth
In a glistening sheen.

Return now sweet Lady
Return to the land
Look down on thy children
Thy own pilgrim band.

We pray for our country
That once was thy dower
Show forth on its people
Thy mercy and power.

Thy mercy to pardon,
Thy power to restore,
That England may yet be
Thy Dowry once more.

For Jesus and Mary
Let this be our cry,
For Jesus and Mary
We'll live and we'll die.

Verses from a Processional Hymn written by Fr Fletcher and probably used in the 1897 Procession from King's Lynn Station on receipt of the Statue from Pope Leo XIII.

Daily, Daily Sing to Mary

Daily, daily sing to Mary,
Sing, my soul, her praises due.
All her feasts, her actions worship
With the heart's devotion true.
Lost in wond'ring contemplation,
Be her Majesty confess'd.
Call her Mother, call her Virgin,
Happy Mother, Virgin blest.

She is mighty to deliver.
Call her, trust her lovingly.
When the tempest rages round thee,
She will calm the troubled sea.
Gifts of heaven she has given,
Noble Lady, to our race.
She, the Queen, who decks her subjects
With the light of God's own grace.

Sing, my tongue, the Virgin's trophies
Who for us her Maker bore.
For the curse of old inflicted,
Peace and blessing to restore.
Sing in songs of peace unending,
Sing the world's majestic Queen.
Weary not nor faint in telling.
All the gifts she gives to men.

Mary of Walsingham

Mary of Walsingham, Mother of Jesus,
pray for thy Dowry, the land that we love:
England has need of thy powerful protection,
pour on thy children thy gifts from above.

> Thou who didst summon thy servant Richeldis,
> Bidding her build to thine honour a Shrine,
> Help us to follow in thy blessed footsteps,
> Framing our lives on the pattern divine.

Countless the pilgrims whose footsteps have echoed
down through the years along Walsingham's way;
countless the prayers that thy children have offered;
Mary of Walsingham, hear us, we pray.

> Many long years saw thy image neglected,
> only a few sought the help of thy prayers:
> Walsingham's Shrine now again in its beauty
> welcomes each pilgrim who thither repairs.

Pray for us then, blessed Mary, our Mother,
Pray for thy children who kneel in thy Shrine,
Pray that thy Son upon England thy Dowry
Pour down His favours and blessings divine.

> So shall we praise thee with ceaseless thanksgiving,
> So shall we sing of thy love and thy power,
> So shall we feel thy protection and comfort
> all through our lives and in death's solemn hour.

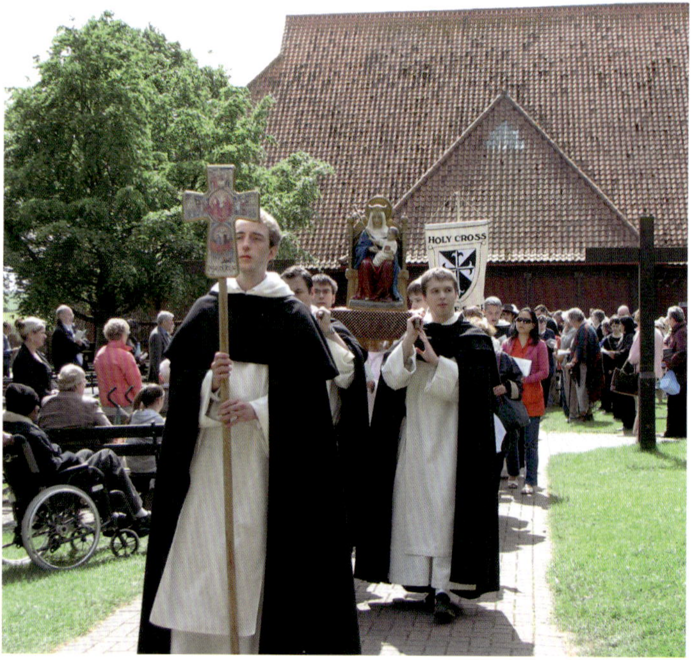
HOLY CROSS

Ave Maris Stella

Hail, thou Star of ocean,
Portal of the sky!
Ever Virgin Mother
Of the Lord most high!

Oh! by Gabriel's Ave,
Uttered long ago,
Eva's name reversing,
Establish peace below.

Break the captives' fetters;
Light on blindness pour;
All our ills expelling,
Every bliss implore.

Show thyself a Mother;
Offer Him our sighs,
Who for us Incarnate
Did not thee despise.

Virgin of all virgins!
To thy shelter take us:
Gentlest of the gentle!
Chaste and gentle make us.

Still, as on we journey,
Help our weak endeavour;
Till with thee and Jesus
We rejoice forever.

Through the highest heaven,
To the Almighty Three,
Father, Son, and Spirit,
One same glory be.

     Amen.

Hail Queen of Heaven

Hail, Queen of heav'n, the ocean star,
Guide of the wand'rer here below;
Thrown on life's surge, we claim thy care:
Save us from peril and from woe.
> Mother of Christ, Star of the sea,
> Pray for the wanderer, pray for me.

O gentle, chaste, and spotless Maid,
We sinners make our prayers through thee;
Remind thy Son that He has paid
The price of our iniquity.
> Virgin most pure, Star of the sea,
> Pray for the sinner, pray for me.

Sojourners in this vale of tears,
To thee, blest advocate, we cry;
Pity our sorrows, calm our fears,
And soothe with hope our misery.
> Refuge in grief, Star of the sea,
> Pray for the mourner, pray for me.

And while to Him Who reigns above
In Godhead one, in Persons three,
The Source of life, of grace, of love,
Homage we pay on bended knee:
> Do thou, bright Queen, Star of the sea,
> Pray for thy children, pray for me.

Lady of Walsingham

Lady of Walsingham, Lady of England,
Look with love on this our land,
Grant us your aid, your prayers and your blessing,
True to our faith we will ever stand.

> *Lady of Walsingham, Lady of England,*
> *Listen to a pilgrim's prayer,*
> *Come back, O Mary, Come back to England,*
> *Back to your Dowry, this island so fair.*

Lady of Walsingham, Lady of England,
Pilgrims all, their love proclaim,
Let the air resound with gladness,
Voices raise to praise your name.

Lady of Walsingham, Lady of England,
Lead us on in the work for peace.
May love and justice guide all nations
War and strife for ever cease.

Lady of Walsingham, Lady of England,
Pray for all in sorrow or pain.
Come back to Walsingham, Nazareth of England,
In the hearts of all to reign.

Consecration to Our Lady

This day, with the whole court of heaven as witness, I choose you, Mary, as my Mother and Queen. I surrender and consecrate myself to you, body and soul, with all that I possess, both spiritual and material, even including the spiritual value of all my actions, past, present, and to come. I give you the full right to dispose of me and all that belongs to me, without any reservations, in whatever way you please, for the greater glory of God, in time and throughout eternity.

Amen.